The Armed Catholic
The Catholic Case for Guns and Self-Defense

By Rick Barrett

While every precaution has been taken in the preparation of this book, the publisher assumes no responsibility for errors or omissions, or for damages resulting from the use of the information contained herein.

THE ARMED CATHOLIC THE CATHOLIC CASE FOR GUNS AND SELF-DEFENSE

First edition. October 15, 2024.

Copyright © 2024 Rick Barrett.

ISBN: 979-8991371414

Written by Rick Barrett.

Table of Contents

Introduction 1
Chapter 1: Is Gun Control a Catholic Issue? 5
Chapter 2: The Modern Church's Opposition to Self-Defense 9
Chapter 3: What Does Tradition Tell Us? 23
Chapter 4: What Does The Church Actually Say? 27
Chapter 5: The Legal History Of Self-Defense 31
Chapter 6: Just War Theory 37
Chapter 7: A Case Of Justified Self-Defense 49
Chapter 8: Conclusion 55

Introduction

The Catholic Church has stood the test of time. From Good Friday to today, she has stood in the breach as the bedrock for Western Civilization. Make no mistake, the Catholic Church from Jesus' parables to her Doctors of the Church has addressed and answered every question on a particular topic. Up to a certain point, ideas and concepts may be questioned, but the ultimate authority of the Church cannot. Unfortunately, modernism has led many to trust in themselves rather than in God. These souls question the hierarchy's every move while surrendering to secular society. Meanwhile, the Catholic Church must constantly defend her positions, sometimes apologizing for not holding the "correct" stance. One of the most stark examples revolves around firearms and their use within Western Civilization. Firearms have long been a contentious issue, with both sides questioning their use. However, our enemy has used this ambiguity to cause doubt and confusion, leading to further division in the One, Holy, Catholic, and Apostolic Church. But how can this be?

Division can occur through the complexity of Catholic doctrine. Catholicism has a rich and extensive body of theological and moral teachings that have developed over centuries. These teachings encompass a wide range of topics, from theology and morality to social justice and ethics. The intricacy and depth of Catholic doctrine can lead to different understandings and interpretations. Visit any social media platform and ask the simple question of "Is the Pope Catholic?" You will receive several different opinions, all claiming to be valid and correct. They will cite different theologians and Bible verses, slandering those who disagree with them. And these are just fellow Catholics! Magisterial Authority is another reason for a growing divided Catholic Church. While the Catholic Church has a centralized authority structure, including the Pope and the Magisterium (the teaching authority of the Church), not all teachings are equally authoritative. Some teachings are considered infallible and binding on all Catholics, while others are open to various degrees of interpretation. This can lead to differing views on the level of authority and interpretation of specific teachings from different groups with a certain agenda. We see this when the question of justified self-defense involving firearms comes up. Because there is no set Scripture verse, commandment or papal decree on firearms, it has left the door open for people to "put their own spin" on the topic. If that spin is supported by the side with the louder outlet, most people will assume their position is correct. Even though firearms usage is not a part of the Church's magisterial teaching, it is assumed to be. So how do we navigate through this controversy?

To navigate this topic, we need to examine the core principles on both sides of the debate. Five principles lay the foundation for discussing the use of firearms in justified self-defense.:

- Sanctity of Life: The Catholic Church strongly emphasizes the inherent dignity and value of every human life. Some Catholics may view firearms as tools that can cause harm or take lives, and as such, they may approach the issue of gun ownership with caution or advocate for stricter regulations to protect human life.

- Just War Theory: While the Catholic Church upholds the principle of nonviolence, it also recognizes the concept of a just war as a means of self-defense and protecting the common good in extreme situations. The Church's teachings on just war provide guidelines for evaluating the use of force in specific circumstances. Some Catholics may grapple with the role of firearms in self-defense, weighing the duty to protect oneself and others against the potential for harm.

- Political Affiliations: Political beliefs and affiliations often intersect with views on the sanctity of life. Catholics with different political ideologies may hold varying positions on issues related to abortion, euthanasia, and other life-related matters. For example, in the United States, Catholic Democrats and Catholic Republicans may have differing perspectives on these issues.

• Social and Ethical Values: Personal social and ethical values, which may be influenced by a range of factors including religious beliefs, upbringing, and personal convictions, can play a significant role in shaping views on the sanctity of life. Some may prioritize the sanctity of life and the avoidance of violence, while others may prioritize personal freedom and the right to bear arms.

• Interpretation of Catholic Teachings in a Changing Social Context: Catholicism encompasses a wide range of teachings and principles on social and ethical issues. Catholics may interpret these teachings in various ways, leading to variations in their understanding of specific moral issues. Because society and culture change over time, Catholics may adapt their ethical values in response to these challenges.

Thus this guide comes into play. As the founder of the Armed Catholic, the first Catholic pro 2A advocacy group, and a firearm enthusiast, this book seeks clarity on the topic of guns rather than imposing my own opinions. We will be looking at the Catholic Church's current stance on self-defense versus what tradition tells us. Next, we will trace the legal history of self-defense in relation to Church teaching as well as examine the concept of proportionality. Finally, we will look at a case of justified self-defense and see how it runs concurrently with Catholic social teaching.

Chapter 1: Is Gun Control a Catholic Issue?

Catholics are not obligated to use firearms or even believe you have the right to use them for self-defense, just like they are not obligated to pray the Rosary or attend weekday Mass. However, this book will reveal that firearms fall within the Church's teaching on justified-defense. Many in our culture today, even Catholics, disagree with this belief as evidence by a 2018 article from USACatholic.org.

In fact, 70 percent of readers agree that gun control is a Catholic issue.[1] Church leaders, especially Bishops, and commentators have continuously held the latter belief. Among the most popular arguments is that one cannot be "pro-gun and pro-life," as if the two were remotely comparable. Others argue that gun ownership makes it impossible to, according to an article written by Richard B. Patterson "embrace the fundamental nonviolence of Jesus' message. There is no denying that Jesus calls us to love our enemy and turn the other cheek. Furthermore, His Sermon on the Mount is a clear invitation to a peaceful lifestyle based on justice and nonviolence."[2] I will use the Republic of Texas as another example of mainstream Catholics resistance to firearms. In 2019, the Texas legislature passed Senate Bill 535, stating that people could "carry guns into churches, synagogues or any other places of worship unless the property owners explicitly prohibit firearms with posted signage."[3] Major dioceses, such as Fort Worth and Dallas, were quick to ban firearms inside the church, with then Dallas Bishop Kevin Farrell stating:

> Texas has become the 45th state to embrace the cowboy mentality that permits the open carrying of guns. It is difficult to see how this new law allowing persons with concealed handgun licenses (CHL) to openly carry firearms can

accomplish anything other than cause people to feel threatened and intimidated.[4]

The crux of these bishops' arguments has always been that the average gun owner will make others uncomfortable, even while following the law. Yet, if someone with ill-intent enters into the house of God, how would those men, who are charged with the defense of their families and those around them, ward off a threat? Yes, you can still defend yourself according to Church teachings. But how can you protect your family if you are already at a disadvantage and have no weapon that can combat the aggressor.

According to Dr. Kevin Miller, moral theologian and assistant professor at Franciscan University of Steubenville: "This is part of the Church's moral teaching, that you have a right to defend your life and to defend the lives of those under your care."[5] The concept of proportionality will be addressed later. But how does the Church's moral teaching align with self-defense, especially with a firearm. When the question of gun ownership in regards to self-defense arises in the Catholic Church, the response tends to be a shrug with the words, "it depends." In 2019, Catholic News Agency interviewed Fr. Thomas Petri, OP and Dr. Kevin Miller concerning the Catholic Church's actual teaching on guns as it relates to self-defense. Fr. Petri said, "It's important to say that firearms...are something relatively modern in the life of the Church and the history of the Church. The Church tends to think in terms of centuries and not in years."[6]

Yes, the Church always looks to her past to properly discern the future. On the other hand, modernity puts the world above the Church's timeless wisdom, thus enslaving mankind. Almost as if the invention of the microwave and the semi-automatic firearm has rendered Church teaching irrelevant. St. Bruno once declared, "While the world changes, the Cross stands firm."[7] Why do we ignore such beautiful truths? Do we not believe that the teachings of the Church are truly universal? The Catholic Church has provided guidance for over 2,000 years, including times when "weapons of war" were swords, bows and arrows and even rocks. I will be citing the Church's perennial teaching in this work to support this claim throughout the rest of this book. Fr. Petri correctly asserts that the church thinks in terms of centuries. And although the tools of self-defense have evolved, the principles the Church teaches continue to apply. Despite the vast history at her fingertips, the modern Catholic Church seems more concerned about modernity than eternity. The Church bureaucracy has worked for the last forty-plus years to convince Catholics that we have no right to bear arms in self-defense.

Chapter 2: The Modern Church's Opposition to Self-Defense

The Catholic Church has the advantage of a long and rich history, especially in the area of self-defense. Hence self-defense it is not a relatively new term. The Church has documentation dating to the Council of Trent in 1566, which the phrase is mentioned and addressed. We have multiple examples of the term "use of force being" applied according to Catholic doctrine. Whether it was the first Crusades (1095-1102) to retake Jerusalem and the Holy Land from Muslim control,[8] the Wars of the Vendée led by Jacques Cathelineau in 1793[9] or the war between The Cristeros and the government of Mexico in 1926,[10] the Catholic Church has never endorsed pacifism. So what happened? When did this dramatic change occur whereby many Catholics in authority have become so rabidly anti-gun?

Can we pinpoint the beginning of this anti-gun sentiment shift? For the United States, the answer seems to be in the 1960's when Liberation theology emerged. Liberation theology is a "religious movement arising in late 20th-century Roman Catholicism and centered in Latin America. It sought to apply religious faith by aiding the poor and oppressed through involvement in political and civic affairs."[11] While Liberation theology sounds very much in line with Church teachings, its roots are far more malicious. According to Ion Mihai Pacepa, a former commander in Romania's communist-era secret police who emigrated to the USA in the late 1970s, Liberation theology was created by the Soviet Union.[12] When asked about Liberation theology and its connection to the KGB, which was the Soviet Union's intelligence agency," Pacepa said:

> *The movement was born in the KGB, and it had a KGB-invented name: Liberation Theology. During those years, the KGB had a penchant for "liberation" movements. The*

National Liberation Army of Columbia (FARC), created by the KGB with help from Fidel Castro; the "National Liberation Army of Bolivia, created by the KGB with help from "Che" Guevara; and the Palestine Liberation Organization (PLO), created by the KGB with help from Yasser Arafat are just a few additional "liberation" movements born at the Lubyanka—the headquarters of the KGB. The birth of Liberation Theology was the intent of a 1960 super-secret "Party-State Dezinformatsiya Program" approved by Aleksandr Shelepin, the chairman of the KGB, and by Politburo member Aleksey Kirichenko, who coordinated the Communist Party's international policies. This program demanded that the KGB take secret control of the World Council of Churches (WCC), based in Geneva, Switzerland, and use it as cover for converting Liberation Theology into a South American revolutionary tool. The WCC was the largest international ecumenical organization after the Vatican, representing some 550 million Christians of various denominations throughout 120 countries."[13]

A main criticism of Liberation theology is that it distills the Catholic Faith to another secular set of political beliefs. As Tom Raabe at *The Federalist* writes:

You pretty much have to become a political leftist to adopt and fully buy-in to liberation theory. Yes, some Christian social-justice warriors deny that politics has anything to do with justice, but that's untrue....Christian social justice activism almost always focuses on racial, gender, poverty and immigrant injustice.[14]

Like every political issue today, whether it is abortion, same sex marriage or immigration, two definitive sides exist within the Catholic

American population. Self-defense is no different. Many Catholic Americans base their understanding of self-defense from their priest's homily versus their own study of the Faith.. Due to time constraints, many Catholics believe it's the Church's job to tell them what they need to know, which is understandable." Unfortunately, this trust has been broken by some Church leaders in order to pursue their own ends. Many U.S. Bishops have spearheaded the charge against firearms by supporting Democratic candidates to sending out tweets favoring individual gun control legislation. As a result, these bishops' voices, these recognizable authority figures, are used by their allies in the political and media spaces to further the anti-gun agenda. Just look at Cardinal Blase Cupich's 2018 statement, "Let us make it clear to our elected officials that the weapons and ammunition that facilitate this carnage have no place in our culture."[15] The good Cardinal is not alone. His statement reflects the majority opinion within the Church's hierarchy, especially visible in the United States Conference Of Catholic Bishops' work (USCCB).

The American Catholic hierarchy's involvement with specific political issues traces back to before the USCCB with the establishment of the National Conference of Catholic Bishops & United States Catholic Conference, both in 1966. Why does this matter? The first reason is that, although Liberation theology did not officially "exist" until 1968 at the second Latin American Bishops' Conference,[16] it has roots in the religious and social movements that swept the Latin American landscape in the fifties.[17] Given its inherent political nature, it would not be a surprise to see Liberation theology in other pastoral documents throughout the world. The second reason is that, if one looks at the goals of both organizations, despite mission statements that appear to focus on addressing the needs of the faithful, they are also worded in such a way that allows for more "involvement" or "evolution" within society. For example, NCCB's goal was that "the NCCB attended to the Church's own affairs in this country."[18] This vague statement, allowed them to encompass anything they wish under the umbrella of "affairs." Now look at the USCCB's mission statement: "the bishops collaborated with other Catholics to address issues that concern the Church as part of the larger society."[19] No one would argue that the Church should take a direct role in society. In fact, one can discern the decay in society with the removal of the Church as its North Star. Unfortunately, the establishment of these groups adds another layer of bureaucracy, and bureaucracy tends to favor centralization and ultimately, authoritarianism.

These groups wasted no time making their true intentions clear. Less than ten years after their formation came the document that has shaped political discourse for American Catholics regarding firearms, and their subsequent use of them. This document is entitled: *Handgun Violence, A Threat To Life—A Statement On Handgun Control*. The United States Catholic Conference (USCC) released it on September 11, 1975. The full restriction on the importation, manufacture, sale, possession and use of handguns is mentioned in this document for the first time. The talking points from this 1975 document will appear in 1990 and 2000 in separate pastoral statements, one directly pulling from the original document and one as a footnote. As we break down the 1975 statement, one will see how the Democratic Party continues to adopt these talking points.

Setting the standard for gun control arguments for the next forty plus years, the statement begins by addressing the number of handguns in the United States (at the time it was 40 million, but this tactic is still used to this day). Shockingly, the second line of the statement says the following: "In most of our cities and rural areas, purchasing a weapon is as easy as buying a camera." The political left continues to use that line today. Just look at the vast array of articles put out by the mainstream media, including such headlines from a 2016 CNN article that states, "It's easier to get a gun than a passport, cold medicine, a divorce and a puppy." The statement continues by introducing the now classic tactic of telling you how many in 1973 died by firearms (28,000) and estimates that 30,000 will die in 1975. Even someone with subpar math skills could see that, 30,000 out of approximately 219,000,000 Americans (which was the population in 1975) translates to .01% of the population at that time. While tragic, it is hardly a statistic worthy of an entire statement from the largest religious group in the country, wouldn't you say?

The document even acknowledges that "gun accidents are now the fifth most common accidental cause of death according to the National Safety Council. In 1973, 2,700 people died in gun-related accidents." Why the emphasis on guns? By their own admission it is the fifth most common, why not focus on the four before it?

The USCC then takes direct aim at gun owners, with this statement:

> *Some have suggested that homeowners and citizens should arm themselves to protect their families from murder, assault or robbery. The sad fact is that a handgun purchased for protection is often used in a moment of rage or fear against a relative or acquaintance. A recent study in the Cleveland area indicates guns purchased for protection resulted in the deaths of six times as many family members, friends and neighbors as intruders or assailants. The 1973 FBI Uniform Crime Report indicates that of all murders almost 25% involved one family member killing another and an additional 40% occur among people who are acquainted.*

Countering the USCC's talking points exposes how politically motivated this document truly is. Let us first address the study that the statement cites. The Cleveland study cited in the1975 document was from Case Western University's medical school. Of the 131 people slain, 114 were family members or friends who died because a gun was in the residence, (of course, this study assumes that because they are family and friends that crimes of passion do not take place or do not count) and

17 were thieves or other criminals. Now let me present a 2022 study by author David Student "People in homes with handguns more likely to be shot dead, major study finds". Although the titles are very similar as to strike a tone of dread, when you look into the actual findings, that just isn't the case. Student actually states "the rates [of homicide] are low." But it was important to consider the increase in a person's risk of being killed, he added. The researchers estimated that over the course of five years, twelve people will be shot to death for every 100,000 people in that circumstance.[20] Next, we need to look at the actual number that is presented. Certainty, every incident involved violence?

Whether it is 1975 or 2022, whenever gun statistics are presented, suicides are included. Taking a look at a Pew Research article from 2022 which stated "A little over half (53%) of all suicides in 2020 – 24,292 out of 45,979 – involved a gun, a percentage that has generally remained stable in recent years."[21] We can compare that to the suicide rate in Japan, a country known for very strict gun control. In the same year (2020), the rate in that country numbered 21,000.[22] Gun control advocates will argue that the presence of a gun plays a factor in whether someone who is in a tortured mental state will take his or her own life. If we compare that to another industrialized Western country like United States, that does not appear to be the case. The tactic of using suicides to increase the number of firearm deaths was first introduced in 1975 by the USCC and has never stopped.

This document introduces another ploy: the government must step in and regulate this "problem" in the form of a National Firearms Policy. Specifically, the document states:

> This is clearly a national problem. No state or locality is immune from the rising tide of violence. Individual state and local action can only provide a partial solution. We must have a coherent national firearms policy responsive to the overall public interest and respectful of the rights and privileges of all Americans. The

unlimited freedom to possess and use handguns must give way to the rights of all people to safety and protection against those who misuse these weapons.

We believe that effective action must be taken to reverse this rising tide of violence. For this reason, we call for effective and courageous action to control handguns, leading to their eventual elimination from our society. Of course, reasonable exceptions ought to be made for the police, military, security guards, and pistol clubs where guns would be kept on the premises under secure conditions.

That line about exceptions being made for law enforcement, military and security guards has been echoed time and time again. Short lived Presidential candidate Michael Bloomberg said at an Alabama political rally in 2020: "But it's the job of law enforcement to have guns and to decide when to shoot. You just do not want the average citizen carrying a gun in a crowded place." The Safe Gun Storage Act of 2021 parrots the idea that guns should be kept under "secure conditions." Nothing is new in the debate over the ownership of firearms; it just gets recycled. Why does the Catholic Church want the government to control their citizens? When did the Church's focus change from saving souls to implementing political agendas?Handgun Violence, A Threat To Life — A Statement On Handgun Control was that moment.. The USCC's document doubles down on the government's importance and how they must regulate their citizens. The document then proposes several steps to control the sale and usage of handguns:

- A several day cooling-off period. This delay between the time of the sale and possession of the handgun by the purchaser should result in fewer crimes of passion.

- A ban on "Saturday Night Specials." These weapons are cheap, poorly made pistols often used in street crime.

- Registration of handguns. This measure could provide an improved system of tracing weapons by law enforcement officials. Registration will tell us how many guns there are and who owns them.

- Licensing of handgun owners. Handguns should not be available to juveniles, convicted felons, the mentally ill and persons with a history of drug or alcohol abuse.

More effective controls and better enforcement of existing laws regulating the manufacture, importation and sale of handguns.

However, the USCC has an ulterior motive behind these steps:

"These individual steps will not completely eliminate the abuse of handguns. We believe that only *prohibiting the importation, manufacture, sale, possession and use of hand-guns, with the exceptions we have already cited, will provide a comprehensive response to handgun violence.*"

This sentiment repeats itself in 1990 and in 2000, even to varying degrees today.

Also, the USCC makes an interesting comparison at the end of their document:

> *We support the legitimate and proper use of rifles and shotguns for hunting and recreational purposes. We do not wish to unduly burden hunters and sportsmen. On the contrary, we wish to involve them in a joint effort to eliminate the criminal and deadly misuse of handguns.*
>
> *We are, of course, concerned about the rights of the individual, as these rights are grounded in the Constitution and in the universal design of our Creator. We are convinced that our*

position is entirely in accord with the rights guaranteed by our Constitution, and particularly with the Second Amendment to the Constitution as these rights have been clarified by the United States Supreme Court. We affirm the traditional principle that individual rights to private property are limited by the universal demands of social order and human safety as well as the common good.

Let's compare that final statement with President Joe Biden's words on June 2, 2022:

For so many of you at home, I want to be very clear. This is not about taking away anyone's guns. It's not about vilifying gun owners. In fact, we believe we should be treating responsible gun owners as an example of how every gun owner should behave.

The more things change, the more they stay the same. The 1975 statement has been the cornerstone for those who have sought to restrict citizens of their God given right to self-defense. Whether in statehouses or in the bishops' office, the playbook to curtail this right remains the same. Yet despite their continued vehement opposition, it has never gone beyond that. The USCCB's best offensive strategy includes a list of archaic recommendations found on their website:

I. A total ban on assault weapons, which the USCCB supported when the ban passed in 1994 and when Congress failed to renew it in 2004.
II. Measures that control the sale and use of firearms, such as universal background checks for all gun purchases.
III. A federal law to criminalize gun trafficking;
IV. Regulations and limitations on the purchasing of handguns;

In addition to these positions, the USCCB has been a longtime proponent of the United Nations Arms Trade Treaty. The USCCB has written to multiple presidents about the adoption of this treaty, which "establishes common standards for the international trade of conventional weapons and seeks to reduce the illicit arms trade."[23] This will be important when we address Pope Francis's comments on firearms. However, the USCC and now USCCB are not the only ones to pursue the disarmament of populations. We can trace their anti-arms stance back to the Vatican.

In a 2011 *National Catholic Reporter* article entitled, "Gun control: Church firmly, quietly opposes firearms for civilians" by Carol Glatz, we are introduced to Tommaso Di Ruzza. At the time of the article, Di Ruzza is referred to as "the expert on disarmament and arms control at the Pontifical Council for Justice and Peace."[24] Di Ruzza is quoted as saying:

> *The Catholic Church recognizes that "states will need to be armed for reason of legitimate defense," as Pope Benedict XVI said in a message to a Vatican-sponsored disarmament conference in April 2008. However, armed defense is something appropriate for nations, not for all individual citizens in a state where rule of law is effective.*

While Glatz states that "According to the Catechism of the Catholic Church, individuals have a right and a duty to protect their own lives when in danger, and someone who 'defends his life is not guilty of murder even if he is forced to deal his aggressor a lethal blow.'" She continues, "How that 'lethal blow' could be licitly wielded is unclear, but the catechism clarifies that repelling the aggressor must be done 'with moderation' in order to be 'lawful' in the eyes of the church; using 'more than necessary violence' would be unlawful, it says." Pretty cut and dry right? In a sense, I agree partially with her statements.

Now Glatz offers her own "Church" interpretation clearly with an agenda.. She claims, "According to the catechism, the right to use firearms to 'repel aggressors' or render them harmless is specifically sanctioned for 'those who legitimately hold authority' and have been given the duty of protecting the community." She is quoting the Catechism of the Catholic Church (*CCC*) #2266. Does that sound familiar? She appears to be quoting the USCC's 1975 Document verbatim. At the same time, she limits the concept of those who hold legitimate authority to agents of the state. Whether this is due to ignorance of the individual laws that govern this union of states or it's intentional, shows her narrow interpretation of the *CCC*.

Glatz returns to Di Ruzza to support her claim. He states that "'a democracy, where there is respect for institutions (of law), the citizen relinquishes his right to revenge onto the state,' which, through its law enforcement and courts system, aims to mete out a fair and just punishment."

In other words, when a country has an effective military, police force, and justice system, you give up any individual right. Di Ruzza doubles down on this example with the following scenario: "Do I still serve the common good (used in the 1975 document) with my gun or do I put it at even greater danger? This infers that any society that has firearms is a lawless society using 'street justice where if you steal my car, I shoot you."[25] Di Ruzza holds a warped sense of justice, because there is no Catholic society, even those with arms, that would encourage such behavior.

Di Ruzza concludes by referencing the Vatican's Justice and Peace Council's 1994 document, which said that "in a world marked by evil and sin, the right of legitimate defense by armed means exists." But Di Ruzza believed it wasn't lauding the potential of weaponry as much as it was lamenting the existence of arms in an imperfect world.[26] It is a shame when people attach emotions to statements rather than just stating the facts.

Di Ruzza makes two statements that are worth unpacking. First, the word, "revenge," then the concept of "those who legitimately hold authority and have been given the duty of protecting the community." First, he uses the term revenge, which is interestingly used in the context of defensive firearm use. To define the word "revenge" is to speak of retaliation which means "to do something in response to an action done to oneself or an associate." Well, this seems to reinforce Di Ruzza's claim above, correct? Let me propose the following scenario: if someone breaks into my home and threatens my family, am I seeking revenge for acting in self-defense? To clear up confusion, let us define what self-defense is. According to Cornell Law, self-defense is defined as "the use of force to protect oneself from an attempted injury by another." I agree full-heartedly with Di Ruzza that Catholics *do not have the right to vengeance*. Vengeance is reserved for God and God alone. As Sacred Scripture declares,

> *Revenge is mine, and I will repay them in due time, that their foot may slide: the day of destruction is at hand, and the time makes haste to come. (Deut. 32:35)*

However, we are not participating in an act of revenge when we experience danger. As stated previously, we have a right and a duty to protect our own lives when in danger. So the issue is revenge versus defense, causing a muddled message. No Catholic who is aware of Church teaching would agree that revenge is a just action.

Second, Di Ruzza states that protecting the community is left to those who hold legitimate authority (Glatz mentions this as well). This is an example of the cultural differences between Europe and these United States. European countries (outside of a select few) restrict firearms to hunting and sport. Furthermore, it is culturally acceptable for only the police or military to have access to firearms, which is far different from our culture.

Some will incorrectly cite the Second Amendment as our "right to keep and bear arms." But it never was and never will be, regardless of what the great Supreme Justice Clarence Thomas says. For example, my right of self-defense comes from God and is protected by Article 1 Section 23 of the Texas Constitution, which states "Every citizen shall have the right to keep and bear arms in the lawful defence† of himself or the State; but the Legislature shall have power, by law, to regulate the wearing of arms, with a view to prevent crime."[27] According to the my state laws, I am given such authority that Di Ruzza says is only reserved to the community. Second, the state of Texas is one of the states that has the supposed controversial "Stand Your Ground Law" or "Castle Law" stating "that you have no duty to retreat when there is a reasonable belief you are in danger and it extends to your home, vehicle, or job. You can justify the use of deadly force if you believe it was absolutely necessary to prevent a violent crime like sexual assault, kidnapping, murder, or robbery."[28] These two laws give the individual, not the state, the duty and obligation for their own self-defense.

Why do we need such laws? As Di Ruzza states, we have police, so there should be no need for personal firearm possession because the police are "authorized" with the protection of the community. Is that true? Not in this union. Law enforcement organizations are not compelled to protect citizens, according to the U.S. Supreme Court.

Two Supreme Court cases, *DeShaney v. Winnebago* and *Town of Castle Rock v. Gonzales,* come to mind. According to the Supreme Court, police departments are not required to safeguard citizens. In other words, even when a threat is obvious, police are perfectly within their rights to decide when to act to protect the lives and property of others. To put this plainly, the police are under no obligation to "protect you." They are agents of the state. This attitude was on full display in May of 2022 when the police waited seventy-three minutes before ending the Robbs Elementary School incident in Uvalde, Texas (the police were actually entrusted with the students' safety). So what can we make of Di

Ruzza's statement? His testimony is broad and overlooks the intricacies of how each individual society addresses the right to self-defense, including firearm use. One society can ban any self-defense weapon while another may fully embrace it. Hence the decision to allow firearms for self-defense must be left to the Catholics who exist in each society while the Church hierarchy must provide a clear distinction between banning guns for self-defense and allowing them. Sadly, Church leaders have only made this topic another dividing point among the faithful. There is one person, the Holy Father, who can bring clarity to this issue. Let's see what he has to say in the next chapter.

Chapter 3: What Does Tradition Tell Us?

The Bishop of Rome's role can be confusing for non-Catholics. Many see the papal tiara, the pomp and circumstance around him and the influence he exerts and believe him to be a dictator with unlimited authority. Although the latter statement is untrue, the Holy Father does fulfill three duties to the Church. He is the Father of Kings, Governor of the World and Vicar of Christ.[29] The confusion centers on papal infallibility. Papal infallibility does not mean that we must believe everything the pope says. Instead, papal infallibility concerns the Church's teaching on *faith* and *morals*; it does not extend to a pope's opinions or even actions. He is only infallible when—finding it necessary to define some teaching of the Church more clearly—he delivers a solemn, official doctrine.[30]

To understand papal infallibility in light of guns, let us look at some recent statements by Pope Francis. In 2018, Pope Francis infamously stated that Christians who invest in arms factories are hypocrites. He also chimed in after the school shooting in Uvalde, Texas.

> *"My heart is broken over the mass shooting at the elementary school in Texas. I am praying for the children and adults who were killed, and for their families. It is time to say enough to the indiscriminate trafficking of arms....Let us all commit to ensuring such tragedies can no longer take place."*[31]

It all comes down to the interpretation of that one word: *Trafficking*. To those who wish to use this statement as a placard to beat us into submission, the mere possession of arms and the sale of arms (such as the Daniel Defense rifle that was used in the Uvalde incident) constitutes trafficking. However, when Pope Francis discusses trafficking, he seems more in line with remarks that he has made in the past such as "the context of international warfare and the global weapons industry, not the American debate over civilian small arms ownership."[32] The pope's statement echoes the Vatican's position on the on things such as the Arms Trade Treaty (ATT) and specifically intended to speak on the legal safe transfer of United States' firearms.

In his 2015 Congressional speech, Pope Francis gave another reason for those against firearms to celebrate:

> *Here we have to ask ourselves: Why are deadly weapons being sold to those who plan to inflict untold suffering on individuals and society? Sadly, the answer, as we all know, is simply for money: money that is drenched in blood, often innocent blood. In the face of this shameful and culpable silence, it is our duty to confront the problem and to stop the arms trade.*[33]

Is the Holy Father referencing gun owners or simply the firearms industry? Not surprising, he attacks a component of capitalism. He always returns to the arms trade. When I buy a firearm, I do not have a plan to inflict untold suffering (remember Di Ruzza and revenge). I am also possessing the weapon for my personal use. So despite what some claim, it would not fall under the category of trafficking. Moreover, Pope Francis's statements on guns are not Ex Cathedra. Pope Francis is also not the only successor of St. Peter to comment on this topic.

Pope St. John Paul II's 1995 Encyclical, *Evangelium Vitae*, offers a different perspective than Pope Francis:

> *Certainly, the intrinsic value of life and the duty to love oneself no less than others are the basis of a true right to self-defense. The demanding commandment of love of neighbour, set forth in the Old Testament and confirmed by Jesus, itself presupposes love of oneself as the basis of comparison: "You shall love your neighbour as yourself" (Mk 12:31). Consequently, no one can renounce the right to self-defense out of lack of love for life or for self. This can only be done in virtue of a heroic love which deepens and transfigures the love of self into a radical self-offering, according to the spirit of the Gospel Beatitudes (cf. Mt 5:38-40). The sublime example of this self-offering is the Lord Jesus himself."*

Pope St. Paul II continues:

> *Legitimate defense can be not only a right but a **grave duty** for someone responsible for another's life, the common good of the family or of the State". Unfortunately it happens that the need to render the aggressor incapable of causing harm sometimes involves taking his life. In this case, the fatal outcome is attributable to the aggressor whose action brought it about, even though he may not be morally responsible because of a lack of the use of reason.*

The crux of Pope St. Paul II argument is found in these remarks "Legitimate (justified) defense can not only be a right but a GRAVE DUTY for someone responsible for another's life, the common good of the family or of the state." And, "Certainly, the intrinsic value of life and the duty to love oneself no less than others are the basis of a true right to self-defense."

In contrast to Pope St. Paul II's detailed explanation, Pope St. Pius X offers an even more simplified response when asked if there are cases when it is lawful to kill:

> "It is lawful to kill when fighting in a just war; when carrying out by order of the Supreme Authority a sentence of death in punishment of a crime; and, finally, in cases of necessary and lawful defence of one's own life against an unjust aggressor."

Where Pope Francis's words are obtuse, never addressing Catholics right to protect themselves, Pope St. John Paul II and Pope St. Pius X reiterate the Catholic teaching that self-defense is not only a right, but a duty. However, nothing these popes have said falls under papal infallibility Cleary, the Catholic Church is more than the Pope (though the pope is the Vicar of Christ) as seen throughout Church history.

Chapter 4: What Does The Church Actually Say?

The Catholic Church has over 2,000 years of history, allowing us to address any question or topic. Self-defense is no different. Since the days of Cain and Abel, mankind has struggled with his fellow neighbor. While many cite Bible verses (Luke 11:21 is a personal favorite of mine) to support their positions, several resources exist to bolster our case for self-defense, including the use of firearms. Let us examine the official Catholic Church teachings regarding the right to self-defense.

Catechism of Trent, 1566 A.D.

If a man kill another in **self-defence**, having used every means consistent with his own safety to avoid the infliction of death, he evidently does not violate this Commandment.

Douay Catechism, 1649 A.D.

Q. 484. Is it not lawful to kill in any cause?

A. Yes, in a just war, or when public justice requires it: "For the magistrate beareth not the sword without cause." Rom. i. 4. As also in the blameless **defence** of our own, or our innocent neighbour's life, against an unjust invader.

Baltimore Catechism, 1891 A.D.

Q. 1276. Under what circumstances may human life be lawfully taken?

1. A. Human life may be lawfully taken:

In **self-defense**, when we are unjustly attacked and have no other means of saving our own lives; ...

Code of Canon Law, 1983 A.D.

Can. 1323 The following are not subject to a penalty when they have violated a law or precept:... 5/ a person who acted with due moderation against an unjust aggressor for the sake of legitimate self defense or defense of another; ...

Catechism of the Catholic Church, 1997 A.D.

2263 The legitimate defense of persons and societies is not an exception to the prohibition against the murder of the innocent that constitutes intentional killing. "The act of **self-defense** can have a double effect: the preservation of one's own life; and the killing of the aggressor. ... The one is intended, the other is not."

2264 Love toward oneself remains a fundamental principle of morality. Therefore it is legitimate to insist on respect for one's own right to life. Someone who defends his life is not guilty of murder even if he is forced to deal his aggressor a lethal blow:

If a man in **self-defense** uses more than necessary violence, it will be unlawful: whereas if he repels force with moderation, his defense will be lawful. . . . Nor is it necessary for salvation that a man omit the act of moderate self-defense to avoid killing the other man, since one is bound to take more care of one's own life than of another's.

2265 Legitimate defense can be not only a right but a grave duty for one who is responsible for the lives of others. The defense of the common good requires that an unjust aggressor be rendered unable to cause harm. For this reason, those who legitimately hold authority also have the right to use arms to repel aggressors against the civil community entrusted to their responsibility.

U.S. Catholic Catechism For Adults, USCCB., 2006 A.D.

Self-defense against an unjust aggressor is morally permitted. There is also a moral duty for the defense of others by those who are responsible for their lives. Self-defense or the defense of others as the goal of protecting the person or persons threatened. Once the threat is eliminated, no further action is required. In such situations, the deliberate killing of the aggressor can be permitted only when no other solution is possible. Any response to aggression must be proportionate to the nature of the threat or the act of aggression.

What was the common thread that ran through these official Church documents from 1556 to 2006? That common thread is this: self-defense is permitted by the Catholic Church. Does that quell the debate between opposing Catholic factions? What does all this history mean when we have a Church hierarchy (including the Pope) that seeks to toss it aside in favor of the current thing? Once again, the Catholic Church has the answer, and it comes from the First Vatican Council, which stated the following:

* Further, all those things are to be believed with divine and Catholic faith which are contained in the word of God, written or handed down, and which the Church, either by a solemn judgment on by her ordinary and universal teaching, proposes for belief as having been divinely revealed.[3]

* Usually when a teaching has been reiterated as true and authoritative by a succession of popes/bishops, we have reason to assume that it is part of the ordinary and universal magisterium, and as such must be believed as faithfully as doctrines that have been solemnly defined by a pope or council.[35]

* When a doctrine of faith and morals has been reiterated again and again, or stated in a way that indicates the pope believes it to be a part of divine revelation (or closely connected thereto) or an authentic interpretation of natural law, then Catholics do not process the liberty of dissenting from that teaching.[36]

The doctrine of self-defense has been reiterated again and again by different catechisms, popes, saints and Church councils. Despite the confusion and current iteration from our Church leaders, self-defense—including the use of a firearm to defend oneself—cannot be dissented from. Tradition remains supreme.

Chapter 5: The Legal History Of Self-Defense

Professor Cynthia Ward at The College of William and Mary published an a 2015 article entitled "Stand Your Ground & Self-Defense." Ward's article discusses the core elements of self-defense. She traces this idea as far back as the seventeenth-century English common-law doctrine.[37] Her thorough breakdown of where the idea of self-defense comes from helps us understand the do's and don'ts. While she focuses on the controversial Stand Your Ground law (a law that allows citizens to protect themselves if they feel their lives are in danger), her research of self-defense's history, with English roots, has relevance for today..

First, she looks at the overall climate surrounding self-defense. She notes that some public and media figures think that Stand Your Ground statutes are a recent development in the area of self-defense law, the result of a fervent lobbying effort by the left's favorite boogie man, the gun lobby. Not quite so. Both the Duty to Retreat (In law, the *duty to retreat*, or *requirement of safe retreat*, is a legal requirement ... that a threatened person cannot harm another in self-defense (especially with lethal force) when it is possible to instead retreat to a place of safety).[38] and the No Retreat (Stand Your Ground) statutes, along with their origins in English common-law doctrine, have coexisted for several hundred years in our legal doctrine.

She adds that self-defense developed in England as an exception to the norm forbidding people from engaging in actions that would cause injury or possibly death to another person in a self-defense scenario. According to popular belief, the English common law strictly enforced a duty of retreat, rejecting a self-defense claim unless the claimant could prove that he or she had their "back against the wall" during a lethal attack. She quotes from William Blackstone's Commentaries, which captures the common view of early English law:

> *[T]he law requires that the person, who kills another in his own defence, should have retreated as far he conveniently or safely can, to avoid the violence of the assault, before he turns upon his assailant; and that, not fictiously, or in order to watch his opportunity, but from a real tenderness of shedding his brother's blood. And though it may be cowardice, in time of war between two independent nations, to flee from an enemy; yet between two fellow subjects the law countenances no such point of honor: Because the king and his courts are the vindices injuriarum [avengers of injuries], and will give to the party wronged all the satisfaction he deserves.*[39]

It is interesting to see how Blackstone's Commentary mirrors teachings that have come from such church documents like The Council Of Trent.

However, the duty to retreat goes too far, forcing the victim to consider the actions of the attacker. The use of force is authorized, only when one's life is in danger.

She continues:

> *Alongside the Retreat rule, the principle of "No Retreat" (what we now call Stand Your Ground), though more limited in scope than its American descendant, was an identified feature of English law at least since the works of Sir Matthew Hale and Lord Edward Coke in the seventeenth century, and both doctrines were a continuing thread in the works of William Blackstone and Sir Michael Foster in the eighteenth century and Edward Hyde East in the early nineteenth century."*

The primary difference between Retreat and No Retreat is the notion of "necessity," a fundamental aspect of doctrine of self-defense from its inception:

The necessity rule permitted a claim of self-defense to homicide only when killing the aggressor was unavoidable that is, only when the defendant reasonably believed that the use of deadly force was the only means of saving life or limb."[40]

Professor Ward concedes that Stand Your Ground was heavily constrained by English common-law doctrine; not every scenario in which a defender was forced to choose between "him" and "me" was deemed a proper case of self-defense. Among the earliest commentators of the English common-law doctrine, two distinguishing scenarios existed:

1. cases in which the defendant's use of deadly force was justified- for example, where a blameless and law-abiding defendant used deadly force to repel an attack from a thief or a burglar who intended to kill or gravely injure him, and
2. cases in which the use of deadly force was merely excused- for example where the defendant either bore some responsibility for the deadly encounter, or had reasonably but incorrectly believed that he or she was faced with imminent threat of death or serious injury and responded with deadly force.[41]

The first scenarios definition of self-defense is consistent with Catholic doctrine. Interestingly, these ideas first gained traction when England was still a Catholic country. The first real application of this idea occurred in 1876 via *Erwin v. State*. The Ohio State Supreme Court wrote that criminal law:

will not permit the taking of [human life] to repel a mere trespass, . . . but a true man, who is without fault, is not obliged to fly from an assailant, who, by violence or surprise, maliciously seeks to take his life or do him enormous bodily harm.[42]

According to Professor Ward, the term "true man" here simply referred to an honorable person who was lawfully going about his business before experiencing a sudden, lethal, illegal, and unprovoked attack. The attacker intended to murder him or inflict serious bodily damage. The Erwin court determined that these honorable individuals may assert self-defense even if they kill the assailant without first attempting to flee in order to protect themselves. She continues:

> *Importantly, in Erwin the Ohio Supreme Court explicitly couched the No Retreat doctrine within the framework of necessity-the principle that a self-defense claim is permitted only when the defendant reasonably believes that killing an aggressor was the only available means of preventing a deadly attack. At the normative level, the Erwin court explained its rejection of the Duty to Retreat no on the basis of discouraging cowardice, but on the basis that the Stand Your Ground rule was "best calculated to protect and preserve human life."*[43]

The Indiana Supreme Court adopted the No Retreat strategy a year after *Erwin v. State*. In the *Runyan v. State case*, John Runyan shot and killed the victim who was harassing him.[44] The jury found him guilty of manslaughter after being instructed to follow a standard that heavily favored the Retreat rule. The jury provided the following relevant details:

> *The law gives to every man the right of self-defence. . . . He may repel force by force, and he may resort to such force as, under the circumstances surrounding him, may reasonably seem necessary to repel the attack upon him, and, in his defence, he may even go to the extent of taking the life of his assailant. The law, however, is tender of human life, and will not suffer the life even of an assailant and wrong-doer to be taken, unless the assault is of such a character as to make it appear reasonably necessary to*

the assailed to take life in defence of his own life, or to protect his person from great bodily harm. And if the person assailed can protect his life and his person by retreating, it is his duty to retreat, And thus avoid the necessarily of taking human life."[45]

Professor Ward then describes other state court cases from the late 1800s that support the No Retreat approach,. Specifically, these cases reaffirm a person's right to use deadly force without first attempting to retreat if:

1. the person is in a place where the person has the lawful right to be;
2. the person is the victim of a deadly and unprovoked attack from which
3. the person honestly and reasonably fears death, grave bodily injury, or commission of a serious felony
4. the person reasonably believes that using deadly force to repel the attack is the only available means of forestalling such injurious consequences. [46]

It's impossible to ignore the Catholic Church's key role in shaping our understanding of self-defense as it pertains to the law, especially if one examines her many past documents. And these documents date back to 1566. Our political opponents have betrayed the Church's illustrious past by molding the contemporary outlook through the lens of modernity. Clearly, St. Thomas Aquinas would have disagreed with the modernists. He wrote,:

Wherefore if a man, in self-defense, uses more than necessary violence, it will be unlawful: whereas if he repels force with moderation his defense will be lawful, because according to the jurists. "it is lawful to repel force by force, provided one does not exceed the limits of a blameless defense." Nor is it necessary for salvation that a man omit the act of moderate self-defense in order to avoid killing the other man, since one is bound to take more care of one's own life than of another's.[47]

Protecting one's own person lies at the heart of self-defense. Sadly, our political opponents overlook this truth when they label us as gun crazy killers. Guns are the only object to have culturally imposed goals, attitudes, and capacities. Owning one automatically makes you seem terrible. In fact, many reasons exist for gun ownership, including, for most Americans, the right to self-defense (as long as the criteria are fulfilled). How can Catholics specifically live out the Church's teachings in regards to carrying a firearm or using it for self-defense in a modernistic culture? The answer seems to be in the form of one of the most popular documents the Church has ever produced, Just War Theory.

Chapter 6: Just War Theory

When recalling the Just War Theory, St. Augustine automatically comes to mind. He focused on the conflict between being a faithful and devout Christian while still being able to meet the demands of living in a world where violence seems to be necessary.[48] He relied on the moral framework rather than the legalistic view when formulating his concept of just war along with using Cicero's idea of right intention in declaring for war.[49] A war must comply with three things in order for it to be considered just according to St. Augustine:

- It had to have a just cause.

- It had to be declared just by a recognized, official authority

- It could only be waged with the rightful intention, to ultimately preserve civil order and lasting peace.[50]

A just war must also be undertaken with the right (moral) intentions in mind. St. Augustine believed this intention should focus on "Christian love" for one's neighbors and enemies alike. A just war should never, and could never be waged out of hatred or revenge. Furthermore, a just war should only be started when good will ultimately result from the use of force. It must be done for the restoration of peace and civil order. [51] For the modern Catholic, the defense of himself, his family and his property can fit within this first prerequisite.

St. Augustine defended the proper use of force under certain circumstances. His classic text laid the foundation for the later Christian understanding of just war. St. Augustine recognized the basic fact that sometimes force must be used to stop the evils of human violence. Later in this text St. Augustine wrote:

> *A great deal depends on the causes for which men undertake wars, and on the authority they have for doing so; for the natural order which seeks the peace of mankind, ordains that the monarch should have the power of undertaking war if he thinks it advisable, and that the soldiers should perform their military duties in behalf of the peace and safety of the community. When war is undertaken in obedience to God, who would rebuke, or humble, or crush the pride of man, it must be allowed to be righteous war; for even the wars which arise from human passion cannot harm the eternal well-being of God, nor even the saints.*[52]

Another Just War passage discusses the ultimate end of those engaged in war, which is peace.

> *"Peace should be the object of your desire; war should be waged only as a necessity...in order that peace may be obtained. Therefore, even in waging a war, cherish the spirit of a peacemaker, that, by conquering those whom you attack, you may lead them back to the advantages of peace...As violence is used toward him who rebels and resists, so mercy is due to the vanquished or captive."*[53]

We can learn much from these few lines.

Our focus here is to apply the concept of Just War to the concept of justified self-defense. First, we will distill the definition of war at a personal level. Then we will examine the three pillars that St. Augustine uses to define what makes a war just. Next, we will apply those to our time period.

When discussing the concept of war, people quickly imagine WWI trench warfare or jets flying across the Vietnamese sky. These images of war are normal because they fit the standard definition of what a war is. After all, Webster's dictionary defines war as "a state of usually open and declared armed hostile conflict between states or nations."[54] But that definition does not fit our discussion. Instead, I will be using the second definition given in Webster's. It entails "a period of such armed conflict"[55] What is conflict? Conflict is defined as "fight, battle, war."[56] When looking at cases when self-defense is called into play, whether it be an armed robbery or a breaking and entering, these are cases of armed conflict, or to break it down further, a fight. Specifically, you have a person, in some cases a group of people, attempting to cause injury to another, whether that be physical in the form of abuse or mental in the form of the destruction of their piece of mind. So with those clarifications in place, we can successfully distill Just War Theory down to the individual level and apply it to our everyday lives. This practical application of Just War Theory offers a necessary moral code to follow when carrying weapons (gun, knife, etc.) to defend ourselves in an increasingly violent society. So how do we apply the three pillars of Just War Theory to our individual lives?

The first pillar is "had to have a just cause." When we look at Just War Theory as it is currently written, it is divided into two different sections: *Jus ad Bellum* (Right to War) and *Jus in Bello (Justice in War)*. Both of these sections lay out different ethical arguments that one must satisfy in order to render a war "just." We can further look at the six criteria that are necessary for *Jus ad Bellum* which are the moral standards for going to war.[57] Remember that the term war has already been associated with combat at the individual level.

1. *Just Cause* – There must be a just and proper reason for going to war. Some of the justifiable reasons include self-defense, protecting the innocent (e.g., preventing genocide), restoring human rights wrongly denied, and assisting an ally in their self-defense.
2. *Proportionate Cause* – The good of going to war must outweigh

the destruction and death that will be caused by warfare. In other words, going to war must prevent more evil and suffering than it is expected to cause.
3. *Right Intention* – Our reasons and motives for engaging in warfare must be noble and in line with the ethic of Christian love. We can go to war to right a wrong or restore a just peace but not to restore our "national pride" or to seek revenge against an enemy.
4. *Right Authority* – War can only be authorized by a legitimate governing authority. This means it has to be a governing authority we would recognize as fitting the criteria of Romans 13. But it also means that the proper governing authority has actual sovereign authorization to engage in war. For example, the President of the United States has the proper authority to initiate warfare against Canada while the governor of North Dakota does not.
5. *Reasonable Chance of Success* – The initiation of warfare brings violence, pain, and suffering. This cost is only worth paying if it will, as we noted, outweigh the destruction and death that will be caused by warfare. If there is no reasonable chance of success in warfare, then there can be no reasonable chance of using warfare to restore a just peace.
6. *Last Resort* – Engaging in warfare must be the last reasonable and workable option for addressing problems. Any peaceful alternatives, such as diplomacy or non-violent political pressure, must first be exhausted before going to war.[58]

Now that we know the criteria for *Jus ad Bellum*, how can we apply this to our everyday lives? Let us take a look at point one :"There must be a just and proper reason for going to war. Some of the justifiable reasons include self-defense, protecting the innocent (e.g., preventing genocide), restoring human rights wrongly denied, and assisting an ally in their self-defense." Within this definition, we see how we can apply it to the individual. If self-defense and protecting the innocent are valid causes to enact violence, then why can't we as an individual operate by this same code? Many states have enshrined self-defense into law in one way or another. As of the writing of this book, thirty-five[59] states have "stand your ground" laws in place. We, as members of specific states within this Union, potentially have the legal justification for use of force for self-defense, which helps it qualify for the first prerequisite of *Jus ad Bellum*. The second part of that initial sentence reads "protecting the innocent." We can use the state of Texas to address this in its Penal Code Section 9.33, "which provides you may protect another person if under the circumstances, as you reasonably believe them to be, you would be justified in protecting yourself, and you reasonably believe your intervention is immediately necessary to protect that person."[60] From the legal perspective, we have fulfilled the first criterion of *Jus ad Bellum*. Let us continue to break down the other criteria.

The second criterion for *Jus ad Bellum*, which would allow us to apply Just War Theory to the individual is *Proportionate Cause*, which states "The good of going to war must outweigh the destruction and death that will be caused by warfare. In other words, going to war must prevent more evil and suffering than it is expected to cause." This poses a challenge. At what point is the use of force absolutely necessary? Frequent debates about proportional response occur within the self-defense community during training and after real life incidents. How long must you wait? How many shots will you fire? Could you have avoided the situation? Unfortunately with as many questions that are raised, you will get almost as many answers. As far as when the threshold is met for you to draw a weapon and use it to defend yourself, no hard and fast rule exists. The standard is also different for men and women. Women may feel unsafe or threatened far sooner than men would. In terms of the actual encounter, could you have avoided it? Perhaps you could have went a different route, locked your doors when you got home, or paid more attention to your surroundings? Or, if faced with a threat, is it really worth going to war for the contents of your wallet or your cell phone? This second qualification really challenges us, especially Catholics, to reflect seriously on what we value in this world and to understand the responsibility we assume when we choose to carry a weapon.

While I am arguing in favor of using force, force is always a *last* resort. None of us want to experience the aftermath of a deadly encounter. Therefore, force must be avoided at all costs. That being said, let us further break down this second criteria: the good of war must outweigh the destruction and death that is caused by going to war. This can be simplified as follows: if someone makes a choice to violate the peace of another, to willingly endanger the life of another, the response to that threat is justifiable. No one on this planet has a right to take your life from you. That is up to God and God alone. For someone to take that step, it is your duty to respond. For spouses, this holds especially true. For parents, this is not even a question. But what does proportionality really mean in relation to modern society?

When speaking of proportionality, one can once again invoke St. Thomas Aquinas, who stated in *Summa Theologiae*:

> *I answer that, Nothing hinders one act from having two effects, only one of which is intended, while the other is beside the intention. Now moral acts take their species according to what is intended... Accordingly the act of self-defense may have two effects, one is the saving of one's life, the other is the slaying of the aggressor. Therefore this act, since one's intention is to save one's own life, is not unlawful, seeing that it is natural to everything to keep itself in "being," as far as possible. And yet, though proceeding from a good intention, an act may be rendered unlawful, if it be out of proportion to the end..*[61]

We live in a society of fallen men who have access to firearms. In theory, as decent human beings, we should be allowed access to the same means of self-defense. Our political opponents (including those who occupy places of Church authority) argue that citizens' legal ownership of firearms should be considered the same as the trafficking of illegal firearms. Here in the United States, however, I fill out a Form 4473 and pay the unjust taxes that the federal government imposes on me in order to exercise this right that God and the state of Texas have bestowed upon me. What part do I play in this, exactly? To what extent am I going against the principle of proportionality if I have access to these firearms, am of sound mind, and have a firm grasp of self-defense doctrine? Let's look at proportionality.

Professor Uwe Steinhoff of the Department of Politics and Public Administration at The University of Hong Kong published a 2017 article titled: "Proportionality in Self-Defense." His article states:

> *"The proportionality of self-defense does not depend on the rights of the aggressor alone, but also on a precautionary rule, shaped by the balance of interests of the society in question and aimed at protecting innocent people and other social interests."* [62]

When arguing about an innocent aggressor (such as someone under the influence of hallucinogenic drugs), Professor Steinhoff addresses a topic dear to Catholics. Specifically, we can run the risk of using too much force on a supposed "innocent" aggressor in self-defense.. The article continues by stating:

> *Abiding by the rule not to harm aggressors unnecessarily will reduce the likelihood that the defender unnecessarily harms innocent people and thereby violates their rights. Insofar as morality requires agents not to impose unfair and unreasonable risks on others, it requires defenders to abide by the necessity requirement. This requirement is thus indirectly based on rights*

> *(though not of aggressors but of innocent people), but violating it is not the same as violating a right. The rationale is also not an overall "rights-utilitarianism" that tries to reduce overall rights-violations: rather the rationale is an agent-relative requirement to take reasonable and fair precautions to reduce one's own likelihood of violating other people's rights. Thus, the necessity requirement is (at least also) a precautionary rule.*[63]

This lines up with Eric Sammons' *Crisis Magazine* article titled, "The Catholic Case for Guns." Sammons writes:

> *Catholics have a duty to protect the innocent. This is particularly true of those who have a vocation to protect their families: husbands and fathers. A man who would allow his wife or child to be attacked without using force—even deadly force—to protect them has failed in one of his fundamental responsibilities. Women, too, are often called upon to protect themselves and others, and should be equipped to do so.*[64]

But how do we measure out proportionality? Is there any rubric to see when we have crossed the line? The proportionality of the force exercised in self-defense should derive from the force used by the attacker.[65] In his book, The *Law Of Self Defense Principles,* Andrew Branca writes, "The element of proportionality is like weight class in wrestling. It wouldn't be a fair fight to ask a 100 pound person to go up against someone who weighs 200 pounds." Branca also describes the modern definition of proportionality in the following way:

> "The force you use cannot be disproportionately greater than the force threatened by your attacker. So, if your attacker is threatening to use only non-deadly force, your response must be limited to non-deadly force."

Of course, this is a fantastic definition, but we must ask ourselves this question: How are we able in the heat of the moment, with our adrenaline pumping, to conceive what is or is not deadly force? Trying to abide by this standard is going to leave the individual frozen in a loop of constant evaluations. They will be paralyzed by indecision, which could seal their fate, and ultimately their life.

But is there anything in the Catholic Church's long and vaulted history that supports the idea of proportionality? Is there any specific rule or part of the Catechism that can guide us? While not in the Church's official documents, St. Augustine's teachings on this matter are critical. Many scholars argue that St. Augustine is the most influential Christian philosopher of antiquity due to his views on social and political philosophy before the Roman Empire's demise. To this day, St. Augustine's impact is long lasting. His writings served as a bridge between the concepts of antiquity and those of the medieval world.[66] Although this may present problems or hesitations when we first read this qualification, once certain circumstances are met we can apply this to our everyday philosophy of self-defense. When we look at many of the other qualifications, this reasoning can also be applied to *Right Intention, Reasonable Chance of Success* as well as *Last Resort*.

The third criterion for Jus Ad Bellum, is Right Intention, which St. Augustine described as "our reasons and motives for engaging in warfare must be noble and in line with the ethic of Christian love. We can go to war to right a wrong or restore just peace but not to restore our "national pride" or to seek revenge against an enemy."[67] To engage in the true art of self-defense is to engage in a noble cause that is conformed with Christian love. It cannot be stressed enough that to engage in the act of self-defense is to defend one's own life or the life of another. In order for this act to be noble, however, it must be a life threatening situation.

The right to authority is the next criterion for the right to war. Specifically, "War can only be authorized by a legitimate governing authority." For most people that would end their ability to use Just War as a personal everyday philosophy. However, the concept of legitimate authority can be distilled down to the individual, at least in the United States. After all, one has the ability to own property and to make their own decisions. And I believe these rights ought to extend to our ability to defend ourselves. Some may argue that this position is akin to vigilantism. That gun owners are going out impersonating superheroes trying to find our own brand of "justice." In reality it could not be farther from the truth. This guide has documented the English common law roots of self-defense from a legal aspect. It has also established how the Catholic Church has extensively addressed this concept from a spiritual perspective. In most states in this Union, people do have the agency and the authority to defend themselves. With this authority comes repercussions for its misuse. Whether it is "Stand Your Ground" or a form of "Castle Doctrine" the approach remains the same. We have also already documented that 'war" can happen at the personal level. We have addressed *Jus Ad Bello*, the criteria that need to be met in order to engage in self-defense (or war). So what is *Jus In Bello* or Justice in War ? These are the ethical principles that govern the way combatants conduct themselves in the 'theater of war".[68] Let's take a look at these criteria:

A. *Discrimination* requires combatants only to attack legitimate targets. Civilians, medics and aid workers, for example, cannot be the deliberate targets of military attack. However, according to the principle of double-effect, military attacks that kill some civilians as a side-effect may be permissible if they are both *necessary* and *proportionate.*
B. *Proportionality* applies to both *jus ad bellum* and *jus in bello*. *Jus in bello* requires that in a particular operation, combatants do not use force or cause harm that exceeds strategic or ethical benefits. The general idea is that you should use the minimum amount of force necessary to achieve legitimate military aims and objectives.

C. *No intrinsically unethical means* is a debated principle in just war theory. Some theorists believe there are actions which are always unjustified, whether or not they are used against enemy combatants or are proportionate to our goals. Torture, shooting to maim and biological weapons are commonly-used examples.

D. *Following orders' is not a defence* as the war crime tribunals after World War II clearly established. Military personnel may not be legally or ethically excused for following illegal or unethical orders. Every person bearing arms is responsible for their conduct, not just their commanders.[69]

While the above criteria are not as impactful as *Jus Ad Bello* is in our personal everyday philosophy, they pertain to the actual act itself (which this book is not dedicated to), we will cover the basics to tie the entire theory together. Let's start with Discrimination, which "requires combatants only to attack legitimate targets." If one is pushed to the extent that they are engaging in war (combat), then it is incumbent on the actor to ensure that the threat is the only obstacle to be engaged. It is also reflected in the fourth universal gun safety rule of "know what is beyond your target." The last thing we want to do is to take an action to protect our own life, only to infringe on someone else's right to life by being indiscriminate with where we choose to direct our response.

The second criterion, Proportionality, has been addressed extensively in this book. The third qualification, No intrinsically unethical means, should not be applicable to us as individual citizens. We are restricted in what we are allowed to use, whether it be only certain types of firearms or restrictions on the length of a knife we are allowed to carry. It is safe to say that if you are engaged in an act of self-defense, the majority of the time you will not be using "unethical means." The final criterion is 'Following orders' is not a defence, which is only applicable to military or law enforcement, outside of extreme circumstances.

As we can see, Just War Theory has been used within the context of international diplomacy. This is because the populace associates war with nations against nations. However, St. Augustine's Just War Theory is applicable to our everyday lives. In fact, the Christian man should be integrating these criteria into their thinking when they make the decision to invoke the right of self-defense. The weight of taking another life is unbearable, even if it meets all the requirements legally and spiritually.

Chapter 7: A Case Of Justified Self-Defense

After looking at the arguments against self-defense and presenting the Church's actual position on self-defense and proportionality, let's look at a case of justified self-defense. Attorney George L. Lyon, Jr, Esq wrote an article entitled: *"Self-Defense Law: The 5 Elements for Justified Use of Force."* In this article, Lyon cites a Maryland case in which a grand jury declined to charge the defendant, Francisco A. Trujillo, concluding that he acted in self-defense. This case is meant to connect not only the subject matter that has been covered in this book, but also demonstrate the principles in a real world setting.

The story starts with Mario Perez, and his girlfriend and his son, who all attended a holiday gathering at Frank Trujillo's house in Montgomery County, Maryland on December 20, 2015. Trujillo lived with his wife and two kids, who were eight and four-years-old. Trujillo worked for a local construction company as the Vice President. Perez had previously worked for the organization where the two met. Trujillo had invited his friend to stay overnight after dinner and drinks.

Perez had a large build. He played football in high school and, after graduating, joined the Marine Corps. He was interested in Mixed Martial Arts (MMA) fighting, according to Mr. Trujillo, and weighed about fifty pounds more than Trujillo. Perez consumed a significant amount of alcohol throughout the evening. His blood alcohol level would be between 0.22 and 0.28 percent according to the toxicological results. This quantity of alcohol is approximately equal to a 200-pound man consuming more than two six-packs of typical beer over a brief period of time. Perez's judgment and logic would have been severely impaired at this point in his intoxication. Indeed, it is conceivable that someone will become unconscious at slightly greater blood alcohol levels, say 0.30 percent.

With at least two prior convictions for DUI, Perez may have actually struggled with alcohol. In fact, during one of his trials, Trujillo had acted as a character witness for him. During their holiday get-together, a dispute over a work-related topic allegedly erupted, according to Trujillo. Perez started to get upset. Perez made a threat to kill Trujillo and his family as a result of the situation's escalation. Trujillo tried to deescalate the situation, but he was unable. While his wife tried to dial 911, he left Perez, got a firearm, and stood in front of his kids' bedroom doors. Perez charged at him, according to Trujillo, who then fatally shot Perez once in the chest.

Police detained Trujillo and charged him with first-degree murder. At first, he was detained for over a week without being released on bail.

On December 29, 2015, Trujillo was granted bond and released. Then, with this event taking place in Maryland, which was in the process of becoming more hostile to the right to keep and bear arms, the prosecution asked the grand jury to prosecute Trujillo for first-degree murder. They claimed that by getting his gun, Trujillo aggravated the situation and that instead, he should have just phoned the police and backed away from the altercation. After hearing Trujillo's testimony, the grand jury declined to bring charges against him, concluding that he acted in self-defense.

As seen by this case, the use of deadly force in self-defense has many aspects. According to Lyon, there are five interconnected factors—*innocence, imminence, proportionality, avoidance, and reasonableness*— which must all be present in order to support the use of lethal force in self-defense. If one looks at these through a Catholic lens, they clearly align with the Church's timeless doctrines. Outside of innocence, the Four Cardinal Virtues line up with these factors:

A. <u>Prudence</u>: skill and good judgment in the use of resource
B. <u>Fortitude</u>: strength of mind that enables a person to encounter danger or bear pain or adversity with courage

C. <u>Temperance:</u> moderation in action, thought, or feeling
D. <u>Justice:</u> the attainment of what is just, especially that which is fair, moral, right, merited, or in accordance with law

In this case, these virtues are clearly depicted. I will argue momentarily that each one of the five is rooted in Catholic teaching. Lyon states that reasonableness is the most important of the five factors both here and in most situations. Stating that "you may use deadly force to stop what you reasonably believe to be an imminent threat of death or serious bodily harm to an innocent person."[70]

<u>Innocence</u>: Perez was the aggressor, putting Trujillo's life and his family's lives in danger. Trujillo and his family were blameless.

<u>Imminence (Prudence)</u>: Trujillo had a good reason to think the assault would happen soon. According to his testimony, Perez threatened to kill him and his family before charging him. In actuality, Perez confronted a man with a gun.

<u>Reasonableness (Fortitude)</u>: Trujillo could deduce that Perez had the potential to cause death or great bodily injury. Perez was fifty pounds heavier than him, a former Marine, and an MMA student. Significantly, Trujillo was aware that Perez was a skilled combatant. Reasonableness incorporates knowledge of an attacker's background, including his violent tendencies and skills. You don't have the right to defend yourself with lethal force against an unarmed attacker. The case where there is an imbalance of force is the exception. As Lyon points out: "Typical examples of disparity of force include a big guy attacking a smaller guy, a man attacking a woman, a healthy person attacking an infirm person, or a trained fighter attacking an untrained person."[71] This reinforces the concept of proportionality.

1. <u>Avoidance (Temperance)</u>: Maryland is a duty to retreat state, which implies that, if it's safe to do so, the victim must flee the threat before employing lethal force. It was not possible for

Trujillo to retreat, notwithstanding the prosecutor's assertion to the contrary. Lyon gives three reasons why avoidance was not possible here:

2. 2.Trujillo was in his own home where there is seldom a duty to retreat.
3. 3.He had protects in the house he could not leave alone with Perez nor maneuver them to safety while under attack.

There is never a duty to retreat if it cannot be done safely.[72]

As Trujillo recalled, the situation seemed to get worse very quickly. Clearly, the prosecutor is using hindsight in criticizing Trujillo for not calling the police earlier in the altercation. Trujillo probably didn't understand he had to act until he recognized how dangerous the circumstance was. As I like to say often, people do not realize that when it goes bad, it goes bad quickly. He likely would have been beaten to death should he have called 911 rather than arm himself. (Bear in mind the average time for emergency response is fifteen minutes). Trujillo left Perez, grabbed his weapon, and kept watch outside his children's bedrooms and did what he could to head off the situation.

<u>Proportionality (Justice):</u> Perez was stopped by a single shot from Trujillo. You may only use as much force as necessary to halt the assault. Anything beyond isn't self-defense; it's a crime. Trujillo stopped using force after the threat was eliminated. Trujillo abided by the necessary requirements placed upon him. Furthermore, we can apply the concept of Substantive Justice, which is the liberal and purposive interruption of laws, in order to do justice—especially where a formal, strict, and narrow application of the law will lead to hardship, absurdity, or injustice.[73] According to the strict interpretation of the laws (and the approach that the prosecution took by applying the first degree statute to his case), Trujillo should have been charged with a crime. With the use of proportionality on Trujillo's part, the substantive approach of justice was applied.

Let's put this within a Catholic context. *The United States Catholic Catechism For Adults* by the U.S.C.C.B says this about self-defense:

> *Self-defense against an unjust aggressor is morally permitted. There is also a moral duty for the defense of others by those who are responsible for their lives. Self-defense or the defense of others as the goal of protecting the person or persons threatened. Once the threat is eliminated, no further action is required. In such situations, the deliberate killing of the aggressor can be permitted only when no other solution is possible. Any response to aggression must be proportionate to the nature of the threat or the act of aggression.*

Only when Mr. Perez became intoxicated, remember that his blood alcohol level would be between 0.22 and 0.28 percent (when the limit in Maryland is .08), did he become an unjust aggressor by threatening to kill Trujillo and his family. Being backed into a position of having to defend his wife and two kids, Trujillo had no other solution. Trujillo demonstrates proportionality by using only one shot to stop the threat. Also, Trujillo's response was proportionate since Mr. Perez was bigger, stronger, and more skilled in the ways of combat. And therefore, Trujillo used the force multiplier (i.e. the gun) to successfully defend his family, which could be argued that he would not have been able to without it. No matter how you look at it, both legally and from the Catholic perspective, Trujillo was justified in his use of force to protect his family.

Chapter 8: Conclusion

The aim of this book is to present the Catholic Church's teaching on self-defense, a teaching that has existed for centuries. As you have read, this is not an open or shut case. While the case can be made that this has not been an issue for the Church to address, that does not mean this is the Church's fault entirely. The principles of Sanctity of Life, Just War Theory, Political Affiliation, Social and Ethical Values, and Interpretation of Catholic Teachings in a Changing Social Context have contributed to this confusion. Rather than provide clarification on issues like self-defense, these ambiguous principles often create even more misunderstanding among Catholics.

Indeed, the Sanctity of Life is one of the bedrocks of Catholicism. Throughout the centuries the idea of "from conception to natural death" was agreed upon by all who shared the Faith. However, with the advent of liberation theology and the advancement of modernity, people have begun to question this very principle. Following the example of the 46th President of the United States and self-proclaimed "Catholic," Joe Biden, who is pioneering the idea that sensible politicians do not impose their religious beliefs on others, many Catholics have "become" pro-choice. This leads them to conflate the idea of "gun violence," a leftist term that shifts the blame from criminals to inanimate objects, with something like abortion.

Furthermore, the Just War Theory has been completely dismantled and repurposed in the age of the "military industrial complex" to comply with the narrative of "protecting America's interest." Social and Ethical Values have been "evolving" since the 1960's to the point where we have priests openly promoting lifestyles that go against the natural order. These "oppressed" groups claim they are overwhelmingly targeted by gun violence, when the facts do not bear that out. Political Affiliations have continued to spur this divide, with their own power and authority as the endgame. Interpretation of Catholic Teachings in a Changing Social

Context has had the most dramatic effect on how we are navigating the current waters around issues in our society. Simply put, the Church has looked to others to lead instead of being Christ's definitive voice on earth. This lapse in leadership has had devastating consequences that will continue to endure long after corrections have been made. All of these things have contributed to the confusion, which this guide hopefully has highlighted.

This book in no way grants "permission" for anyone to shoot another person—that is not the point. The point is that the Catholic Church has a long and storied tradition on almost every topic that we face today, and the concept of self-defense is one of these areas covered. While nothing in the Catholic Church's teachings say you can use a firearm, it specifically does not say that you cannot! What I can tell you is that you are a precious gift, body and soul which is worth defending. I will end by reiterating what St. Augustine of Hippo once wrote:

"Though defensive violence will always be 'a sad necessity' in the eyes of men of principle, it would be still more unfortunate if wrongdoers should dominate just men."[74]

[1] Sanna, Emily. 2018. "Should Catholics Own Guns?" U.S. Catholic. July 10, 2018. https://uscatholic.org/articles/201807/should-catholics-own-guns/.

[2] PhD, Richard B. Patterson. 2020. "Catholics and Gun Control." Franciscan Media. October 4, 2020. https://www.franciscanmedia.org/st-anthony-messenger/september-2020/catholics-and-gun-control/.

[3] Reporter, Benjamin Fearnow Media. 2019. "Texas Now Allows Guns in Churches, Schools after Firearm Access Expansion." Newsweek. September 1, 2019. https://www.newsweek.com/texas-gun-laws-september-1-effect-schools-churches-restrictions-1457123.

[4] Hicap, Jonah. 2016. "Pro-Gun Catholics Upset at Dallas Catholic Diocese's Decision to Ban Guns in Churches." Www.christiantoday.com. January 17, 2016. https://www.christiantoday.com/article/pro.gun.catholics.upset.at.dallas.catholic.dioceses.decision.to.ban.guns.in.churches/76719.htm.

[5] Farrow, Mary. 2019. "What the Church Does - and Does Not - Teach about Gun Control." Catholic News Agency. Catholic News Agency. August 8, 2019. https://www.catholicnewsagency.com/news/41989/what-the-church-does-and-does-not-teach-about-gun-control%C2%A0.

[6] Farrow, Mary. 2019. "What the Church Does - and Does Not - Teach about Gun Control." Catholic News Agency. Catholic News Agency. August 8, 2019. https://www.catholicnewsagency.com/news/41989/what-the-church-does-and-does-not-teach-about-gun-control%C2%A0.

[7] Jackle, Mary. 2022. "Daily Meditation for April 13, 2022." Saint Benedict's Monastery. April 13, 2022. https://sbm.osb.org/2022/04/13/daily-meditation-for-april-13-2022/.

[8] Cartwright, Mark. 2018. "First Crusade." World History Encyclopedia. July 9, 2018. https://www.worldhistory.org/First_Crusade/.

[9] "Wars of the Vendée | French History." n.d. Encyclopedia Britannica. https://www.britannica.com/event/Wars-of-the-Vendee.

[10] "History of the Cristiada." n.d. Www.laits.utexas.edu. https://www.laits.utexas.edu/jaime/cwp5/crg/english/history/.

[11] Britannica. 2019. "Liberation Theology | Roman Catholicism | Britannica." In *Encyclopædia Britannica*. https://www.britannica.com/topic/liberation-theology.

[12] CNA. n.d. "Former Soviet Spy: We Created Liberation Theology." Catholic News Agency. https://www.catholicnewsagency.com/news/31919/former-soviet-spy-we-created-liberation-theology.

[13] CNA. n.d. "Former Soviet Spy: We Created Liberation Theology." Catholic News Agency. https://www.catholicnewsagency.com/news/31919/former-soviet-spy-we-created-liberation-theology.

[14] Raabe, Tom. 2020. "5 Major Reasons Liberation Theology Is Terrible Theology." The Federalist. October 12, 2020. https://thefederalist.com/2020/10/12/5-major-reasons-liberation-theology-is-terrible-theology/.

[15] How the Catholic Church could help lead a gun control movement. 2018. "How the Catholic Church Could Help Lead a Gun Control Movement." America Magazine. February 21, 2018. https://www.americamagazine.org/politics-society/2018/02/21/how-catholic-church-could-help-lead-gun-control-movement.

[16] Britannica. 2019. "Liberation Theology | Roman Catholicism | Britannica." In *Encyclopædia Britannica*. https://www.britannica.com/topic/liberation-theology.

[17] Hillar, H, and Marian Hillar. 1993. "LIBERATION THEOLOGY: RELIGIOUS RESPONSE to SOCIAL PROBLEMS. A SURVEY Published in Humanism and Social Issues. Anthology of Essays." *American Humanist Association*. https://socinian.org/files/LiberationTheology.pdf.

[18] "About Us | USCCB." n.d. Www.usccb.org. https://www.usccb.org/about.

[19] "About Us | USCCB." n.d. Www.usccb.org. https://www.usccb.org/about.

[20] agencies, Guardian staff and. 2022. "People in Homes with Handguns More Likely to Be Killed, Major Study Finds." The Guardian. April 7, 2022. https://www.theguardian.com/us-news/2022/apr/07/guns-handguns-safety-homicide-killing-study.

[21] Gramlich, John. 2023. "What the Data Says about Gun Deaths in the U.S." Pew Research Center. Pew Research Center. April 26, 2023. https://www.pewresearch.org/short-reads/2023/04/26/what-the-data-says-about-gun-deaths-in-the-u-s/.

[22] "Japan: Number of Suicides 2019." 2022. Statista. March 2022. https://www.statista.com/statistics/622065/japan-suicide-number/.

[23] "The Arms Trade Treaty at a Glance | Arms Control Association." 2019. Armscontrol.org. 2019. https://www.armscontrol.org/factsheets/arms_trade_treaty.

[24] "Gun Control: Church Firmly, Quietly Opposes Firearms for Civilians." n.d. National Catholic Reporter. Accessed November 1, 2023. https://www.ncronline.org/gun-control-church-firmly-quietly-opposes-firearms-civilians.

25 "Gun Control: Church Firmly, Quietly Opposes Firearms for Civilians." n.d. National Catholic Reporter. Accessed November 1, 2023. https://www.ncronline.org/gun-control-church-firmly-quietly-opposes-firearms-civilians.

26 "Gun Control: Church Firmly, Quietly Opposes Firearms for Civilians." n.d. National Catholic Reporter. Accessed November 1, 2023. https://www.ncronline.org/gun-control-church-firmly-quietly-opposes-firearms-civilians.

27 "THE TEXAS CONSTITUTION ARTICLE 1. BILL of RIGHTS." n.d. Statutes.capitol.texas.gov. Accessed November 1, 2023. https://statutes.capitol.texas.gov/Docs/CN/htm/CN.1/CN.1.23.htm.

28 "What Is Stand Your Ground Law in Texas?" 2018. Simer & Tetens. September 19, 2018. https://simerlaw.com/what-is-stand-your-ground-law-in-texas/.

29 2022. Vatican.va. 2022. https://www.vatican.va/news_services/press/documentazione/documents/sp_ss_scv/insigne/triregno_en.html.

30 Shrader, Rachel. 2023. "Pope Infallibility: Myths and Truths." Get FedTM. March 28, 2023. https://www.catholiccompany.com/getfed/catholics-believe-everything-the-pope-says/.

31 CNA. n.d. "Pope Francis: 'My Heart Is Broken' over Texas School Shooting." Catholic News Agency. Accessed November 1, 2023. https://www.catholicnewsagency.com/news/251357/pope-francis-my-heart-is-broken-over-texas-elementary-school-shooting.

32 MacGuill, Dan. 2018. "Did Pope Francis Say Gun Owners 'Can't Call Themselves Christians Anymore'?" Snopes. May 9, 2018. https://www.snopes.com/fact-check/pope-francis-gun-owners/.

33 "Pope Francis' Address to Congress (as Prepared for Delivery) | CNN Politics." 2015. CNN. September 24, 2015. https://www.cnn.com/2015/09/24/politics/pope-francis-congress-speech/index.html.

34 Storck, Thomas, and Peter A Kwasniewski. 2017. *An Economics of Justice & Charity : Catholic Social Teaching : Its Development and Contemporary Relevance*. Kettering, Ohio: Angelico Press.

35 Storck, Thomas, and Peter A Kwasniewski. 2017. *An Economics of Justice & Charity : Catholic Social Teaching : Its Development and Contemporary Relevance*. Kettering, Ohio: Angelico Press.

36 Storck, Thomas, and Peter A Kwasniewski. 2017. *An Economics of Justice & Charity : Catholic Social Teaching : Its Development and Contemporary Relevance*. Kettering, Ohio: Angelico Press.

37 Ward, Cynthia. n.d. "'Stand Your Ground' and Self Defense Article 'Stand Your Ground' and Self-Defense." Accessed November 1, 2023. https://scholarship.law.wm.edu/cgi/viewcontent.cgi?referer=&httpsredir=1&article=2841&context=facpubs.

38 "What Is DUTY to RETREAT and How Does It Work?" 2021. U.S. LawShield. December 30, 2021. https://www.uslawshield.com/duty-to-retreat/.

39 Ward, Cynthia. n.d. "'Stand Your Ground' and Self Defense Article 'Stand Your Ground' and Self-Defense." Accessed November 1, 2023. https://scholarship.law.wm.edu/cgi/viewcontent.cgi?referer=&httpsredir=1&article=2841&context=facpubs.

40 Ward, Cynthia. n.d. "'Stand Your Ground' and Self Defense Article 'Stand Your Ground' and Self-Defense." Accessed November 1, 2023. https://scholarship.law.wm.edu/cgi/viewcontent.cgi?referer=&httpsredir=1&article=2841&context=facpubs.

41 Ward, Cynthia. n.d. "'Stand Your Ground' and Self Defense Article 'Stand Your Ground' and Self-Defense." Accessed November 1, 2023. https://scholarship.law.wm.edu/cgi/viewcontent.cgi?referer=&httpsredir=1&article=2841&context=facpubs.

42 Ward, Cynthia. n.d. "'Stand Your Ground' and Self Defense Article 'Stand Your Ground' and Self-Defense." Accessed November 1, 2023. https://scholarship.law.wm.edu/cgi/viewcontent.cgi?referer=&httpsredir=1&article=2841&context=facpubs.

43 Ward, Cynthia. n.d. "'Stand Your Ground' and Self Defense Article 'Stand Your Ground' and Self-Defense." Accessed November 1, 2023. https://scholarship.law.wm.edu/cgi/viewcontent.cgi?referer=&httpsredir=1&article=2841&context=facpubs.

44 *Runyan v. State*, 705 N.W.2d 107 (Iowa Ct. App. 2005)

45 Ward, Cynthia. n.d. "'Stand Your Ground' and Self Defense Article 'Stand Your Ground' and Self-Defense." Accessed November 1, 2023. https://scholarship.law.wm.edu/cgi/viewcontent.cgi?referer=&httpsredir=1&article=2841&context=facpubs.

46 Ward, Cynthia. n.d. "'Stand Your Ground' and Self Defense Article 'Stand Your Ground' and Self-Defense." Accessed November 1, 2023. https://scholarship.law.wm.edu/cgi/viewcontent.cgi?referer=&httpsredir=1&article=2841&context=facpubs.

47 Saint Thomas Aquinas, *Summa Theologiae*, II-II, q. 64, a. 7

[48] Amell, Amaya. "The Theory of Just War and International Law: From Saint Augustine, through Francisco de Vitoria, to Present." *Hispanic Journal*, vol. 38, no. 1, 2017, pp. 63–76. *JSTOR*, https://www.jstor.org/stable/26535329. Accessed 20 June 2023.

[49] Amell, Amaya. "The Theory of Just War and International Law: From Saint Augustine, through Francisco de Vitoria, to Present." *Hispanic Journal*, vol. 38, no. 1, 2017, pp. 63–76. *JSTOR*, https://www.jstor.org/stable/26535329. Accessed 20 June 2023.

[50] Amell, Amaya. "The Theory of Just War and International Law: From Saint Augustine, through Francisco de Vitoria, to Present." *Hispanic Journal*, vol. 38, no. 1, 2017, pp. 63–76. *JSTOR*, https://www.jstor.org/stable/26535329. Accessed 20 June 2023.

[51] Amell, Amaya. "The Theory of Just War and International Law: From Saint Augustine, through Francisco de Vitoria, to Present." *Hispanic Journal*, vol. 38, no. 1, 2017, pp. 63–76. *JSTOR*, https://www.jstor.org/stable/26535329. Accessed 20 June 2023.

[52] Augustine, *Reply to Faustus the Manichaean* XXII. 75. *NPNF* 4, p. 301.

[53] Bill. 2014. "JUST WAR DOCTRINE." Catholic League. 2014. https://www.catholicleague.org/just-war-doctrine/.

[54] Merriam-webster. 2019. "Definition of War." Merriam-Webster.com. 2019. https://www.merriam-webster.com/dictionary/war.

[55] Merriam-webster. 2019. "Definition of War." Merriam-Webster.com. 2019. https://www.merriam-webster.com/dictionary/war.

[56] Merriam-Webster. 2009. "Definition of Conflict." Merriam-Webster.com. 2009. https://www.merriam-webster.com/dictionary/conflict.

[57] Agency, Mere. 2017. "A Brief Introduction to the Just War Tradition: Jus Ad Bellum - ERLC." Https://Erlc.com/. August 17, 2017. https://erlc.com/resource-library/articles/a-brief-introduction-to-the-just-war-tradition-jus-ad-bellum/.

[58] Agency, Mere. 2017. "A Brief Introduction to the Just War Tradition: Jus Ad Bellum - ERLC." Https://Erlc.com/. August 17, 2017. https://erlc.com/resource-library/articles/a-brief-introduction-to-the-just-war-tradition-jus-ad-bellum/.

[59] "Stand Your Ground (35 States) vs. Duty to Retreat (15 States)." n.d. Reason.com. https://reason.com/volokh/2020/12/21/duty-to-retreat-35-states-vs-stand-your-ground-15-states/.

[60] "Good Samaritan Law in Texas: Be Careful Who You Save." 2019. U.S. LawShield. February 4, 2019. https://www.uslawshield.com/defense-another-texas/.

[61] "SUMMA THEOLOGIAE: Murder (Secunda Secundae Partis, Q. 64)." n.d. Www.newadvent.org. https://www.newadvent.org/summa/3064.htm#article7.

[62] Steinhoff, Uwe. 2017. "Proportionality in Self-Defense." Social Science Research Network. Rochester, NY. January 14, 2017. https://papers.ssrn.com/sol3/papers.cfm?abstract_id=2916988.

[63] Steinhoff, Uwe. 2017. "Proportionality in Self-Defense." Social Science Research Network. Rochester, NY. January 14, 2017. https://papers.ssrn.com/sol3/papers.cfm?abstract_id=2916988.

[64] "The Catholic Case for Guns." 2021. Crisis Magazine. December 10, 2021. https://crisismagazine.com/opinion/the-catholic-case-for-guns.

[65] "Published by the Stockton Center for International Law." n.d. https://digital-commons.usnwc.edu/cgi/viewcontent.cgi?article=2988&context=ils.

[66] Amell, Amaya. "The Theory of Just War and International Law: From Saint Augustine, through Francisco de Vitoria, to Present." Hispanic Journal, vol. 38, no. 1, 2017, pp. 63–76. JSTOR, https://www.jstor.org/stable/26535329. Accessed 20 June 2023.

[67] Agency, Mere. 2017. "A Brief Introduction to the Just War Tradition: Jus Ad Bellum - ERLC." Https://Erlc.com/. August 17, 2017. https://erlc.com/resource-library/articles/a-brief-introduction-to-the-just-war-tradition-jus-ad-bellum/.

[68] The Ethics Centre. 2016. "Just War Theory - the Ethics Centre." THE ETHICS CENTRE. July 19, 2016. https://ethics.org.au/ethics-explainer-just-war/.

[69] The Ethics Centre. 2016. "Just War Theory - the Ethics Centre." THE ETHICS CENTRE. July 19, 2016. https://ethics.org.au/ethics-explainer-just-war/.

[70] Attorneys, Arsenal. n.d. "Self-Defense Law: The 5 Elements for Justified Use of Force." Www.arsenalattorneys.com. https://www.arsenalattorneys.com/firearms-blog/self-defense-case-study-frank-trujillo.

[71] Attorneys, Arsenal. n.d. "Self-Defense Law: The 5 Elements for Justified Use of Force." www.arsenalattorneys.com. https://www.arsenalattorneys.com/firearms-blog/self-defense-case-study-frank-trujillo.

[72] Attorneys, Arsenal. n.d. "Self-Defense Law: The 5 Elements for Justified Use of Force." www.arsenalattorneys.com. https://www.arsenalattorneys.com/firearms-blog/self-defense-case-study-frank-trujillo.

73 "Difference between Procedural and Substantive Justice - LawGlobal Hub." 2019. April 27, 2019. https://www.lawglobalhub.com/the-difference-between-procedural-justice-and-substantive-justice/.

74 City of God, Book IV, Ch. 15

About the Author

Rick Barrett is originally from the state of Rhode Island to the state of Texas at the age of 27. He had never shot a firearm until one fateful day in 2008 and has ignited a passion for all things firearms and self-defense. He founded The Armed Catholic in 2021 to provide first class firearm training on a foundation of Catholic tradition. He is certified from the Untied States Conceal Carry Association as a firearm instructor as well as the State Of Texas as a License To Carry Instructor. He has a Master's from Penn State University and been married to his wife since 2010

Read more at www.thearmedcatholic.com.

www.ingramcontent.com/pod-product-compliance
Lightning Source LLC
Chambersburg PA
CBHW070209100426
42743CB00013B/3111